Loving All

poems by Suzie Palmer

Cyberwit.net, Allahabad, India

2014

ISBN 978-81-8253-137-6

1st Edition: 2009, 2nd Edition: 2009, 3rd Edition 2011, 4th Edition 2014
Rs. 150/-

Cover design: The Shree Yantra is a tool of illumination known to usher peace, prosperity, harmony, and tidings of great joy.

Cyberwit.net
HIG 45 Kaushambi Kunj, Kalindipuram
Allahabad - 211011 (U.P.) India
http://www.cyberwit.net

Tel: (91) 9415091004
E-mail: cyberwit@rediffmail.com / info@cyberwit.net

Printed in India.

Dedication

To my Mum and Dad ~ these poems describe my love and gratitude. Greatest love to those who read these words, to all living beings, and to our Divinity: the source of all inspiration and motivation. *Namaste!*

The Author

Suzie Palmer began writing her life story and poetry in 1999 at 28 years of age. She was encouraged to write after a mystical encounter with a unique Indian sage. *'You are a writer; you must write'* he told her *'you must write about your life – true truth – a story describing this is how I won this battle. People like reading about other people's lives, and they'll like reading about yours. You'll also write poetry, teaching people how to be happy even if they can't run and jump'*. Suzie began writing with great enthusiasm and optimism, knowing that her Multiple Sclerosis (MS) condition was a 'great blessing', helping her to re-remember her life's purpose. She also strongly believes her MS will heal naturally and she pursues this alternative avenue, documenting her healing ventures for the benefit of all.

Her autobiography reveals how a once happy girl becomes even happier despite her physical problem, when she experiences spiritual understanding and liberation. Suzie's life changes forever and she develops altruistic qualities to help better other lives and the world.

Amid her physical problems and healing plight, Suzie has difficultly finding solace in human love. This is where her true agony lies. She describes her relationships with direct honesty, and finds her greatest challenge in writing about her life without hurting others. Her quest for love is universally shared, along with the problems encountered in duality.

In 2002, Suzie wrote her first children's stories of the *Come Fly With Me* series and visited local primary schools between 2002 and 2006 to share them with Year 3 to 6 children. Suzie conducts motivational talks to high school students, presents to mature aged students, and gives motivational talks to adults, to help lift them out of bouts of complacency.

In 2005, Suzie began prolifically writing poetry and posting her poems on authorsden.com—an international writing and poetry site. Suzie has presented some of her poems in public, and receives encouragement from Poet Gatherings.

Suzie sends messages of love to everyone. Inspired by the light of love in people's eyes, Suzie gives much of her time to people in need. *To help make this world a better place* is Suzie's writing drive, and her poems and life reflect this passion.

As well as writing poems, Suzie's central life work is her autobiography, and she looks forward to sharing this with the world.

To view more of Suzie's works see: http://www.authorsden.com/suziepalmer

Or visit: suziepalmer.com

Contents

Shine

Beauty held in the past
To the eyes may not last
The eyes they can and do deceive
When once was obvious is hard to see

True beauty shines beyond
All time
Of actions showing beauty fine
In all we do, that's who we are
It's our ability to shine like stars

The longer we gleam
The more brilliant we are
Entirely gifted to guide a star
From small sparks able to shine
Wisdom and light on humankind

~~~
~~~

Human Might

How to express oneself I ask
Live with a face unmasked
Reveal true colours
Beyond any fable, that everything is good and stable

Risking face
Is a risky trail
Speaking truth because one is able
To live without fear for what is right
Equality in Human Might

Time is here for us to bow
Our dreams of oneness can come true now
It's in our reach to make it happen
Non-separation, a family haven

May the world bridge again
Our earth, our home, our living kin
Everywhere, *there we are*
All parts of nature, near and far

~~~
~~~

Dive into my mind

I'm seeking the experience
Of transcendental illuminance
Divinity inside this holy space
Built by loving sacred grace

In this place revealing our true face
Time as we know it will stand still
Lines are softened, tones in tune
Loving is loving
And true is true

Trying to find it in this world
Is oh so difficult even when you're heard
Yet we must seek it, this we do
Heaven really is in me and you

Dismiss all else, that's our challenge
Identify with elevated balance
Rational thinking is so key
Emotions hamper so easily

I need to dive into my mind
Then far beyond
The heart, my chime
Deep into a swirling mist
Mysticism showing bliss
Our true natures
We are free
To love each other
Let it be

~~~
~~~

My kin, my Friend

All in this together
You and I
With souls united
We can reach
The sky
Of our mind
We will climb in deep
Rekindle passions
Embedded in our keep

Sharing hearts
Each other's spark
We'll guide ourselves
Out of the dark
Into the light
Love's home again
It's great to see you
My kin, my friend
Now, it's time to live again

~~~
~~~

Peaceful Shelter

Writing a poem or two
Is a pleasure to do
If only they could get into
Places that need them to

Where people are suffering and dying
If these words could stop them crying
Ease their troubles, we'll go flying
Imagine life is not so trying

Holding hands, we'll reach the stars
Gather strands of golden sparks
Embrace our family
Near and far
Bundle us in one global car

Takes us to a land that's giving
A peaceful shelter
All foods brimming
In creativity we'll go swimming
Goodness of humankind
Alive and Living

~~~
~~~

Everyday Stars

The artist within
Has always been
Although years have ushered
Her away

Suppressed and quenched
Her artistic bent
Creativity ran astray

Let logic in
To suit, to win
The teachers
Hold the sway

They teach to tell
Academics so well
Dismissing the very thing

That fills our heart
With life, with joy
That makes us who we are
That shines within the light inside
Merging to make us a star!

~~~
~~~

Keep on keeping on

Keep on keeping on
That's what we're here to do
Never give up on life
This gift for me and you

Saints are people who never give up
Keep trying through and through
They know just how to fill the cup
Overflowing love is their homebrew

Keep on keeping on
Raise your face to the sun
Bow to the heavens and the stars
Take breaths full of grace and fun

~~~
~~~

The Mind

The mind
The mind of every kind
Is sensitive
It's true

Potentially
It knows no bounds
Awareness
Sees right through

When awake
It liberates
Everything we do

Infiltrating beauty
Becomes our duty
Creating peace
For us
That's true

~~~
~~~

Moonlight

O moonlight moonlight
Shine your love right over us
To light up our way

Moonlight shines on the night
Hinting of the day
Allows a peek
At what's usually bleak
Dark and hidden away

It shines in time
Around all kind
Lunacy has its say
Lunar she is
Her rays are a bridge
Between light and disarray

If only we could always see it
In darkness
Imbue it
Enlighten our every thought
Take breaths full of grace
For the human race
Moonlight is really a force

For the mind,
Moonlight is kind
Signalling a peaceful resort
Everyone can go there
In a moment

We are there
Moonlight lightens our walk

Call on the light
Of the moon tonight
Even when she's away
Her light is within you
Inside every sinew
Guiding and beaconing
Your way

~~~
~~~

Imagine a Time

Bring on the time
Of loving sublime
Living in a kingdom
Not for the blind

Bring on this time
Where humans are kind
Living fearlessly
Peace can shine

Could this time be now?
Can we possibly change?
Is loving-kindness so far out of range?

If we imagine it
Ripples arise
Effecting the world
Less otherwise

~~~
~~~

To fulfil our purpose

Effort in action
Brings to satisfaction
Amount of exertion
Instilled

Rewards
Are sourced
Par for the course
Reaped from what we do

To fulfil our purpose
Bring to the surface
Passions hidden away

Secrets uncovered
May be keys to discover
Our love, our work, our play

~~~
~~~

A Great Display

All these moments are sacred
I said to myself just then
Even the seemingly little ones
Abiding in action suspend

The ones between the moments
When things may happen, and then
We find ourselves back in quiet moments
There, time can be a friend

Take these moments
With all our presence
The breath will lead the way
Guiding our minds between two worlds
Entering and exiting
A Great Display

~~~
~~~

Something for You

Where is that something for you?
That special thing
Inspiring you
To do
Things you never thought
Able to
Like fly
In your
Mind
From loving sublime
Seeking the Divine
In humankind

What is that something
You wanted to be?
Are you creating
Your sanity?
Truly following brilliancy
By building bridges
Of Liberty

~~~
~~~

Secret Language

Know a person by what you say around them
The wise Sufis say
Listen to your language, your body,
Displays

Know a person by what you *don't* say around them
This, they also say
Recognise what you reveal
What you hide away

Let your ear lead you to your lover
Sound will guide the way
Who is it that soothes your heart?
A certain kind of way

Secrets can be discovered
In our everyday
Open our minds to find them
Sensitive intuition
Has the say

~~~
~~~

Love is the Healer

Love is the world in all its diversity
Living and learning
With others
Life's university

Love is the freedom of all others
We must love
Us
Our sisters and brothers

Love is the pursuing of our dreams
Together
We have a purpose
You and me

Love is all people: soul's united
No separation
Combination
Our lives bind us

Love is the healer
And the king
Hero and the reason
Of all things

Love is a blessing
Its beat is true
The heart is our instrument
To work magic through

~~~
~~~

This beautiful moment

This beautiful moment
Empty and full
There's nothing to it
If we don't pursue
See what's there
Inside it all
In philosophy
The mind enthrals
Then go deeper
To the bone
Observe sensations
On your fingers and toes
Vibrations rise
Then they fall
Guiding us to see it all
Everything changes
Nature shows
From moment to moment
We constantly grow
Each one is a blessing
A present, it's true
Accept this gift for me and you

~~~
~~~

Our Bodies' Cloak

In between moments
Spaces and time
Feels suspended
In the mind

Who are we?
Am I here?
I don't see my face looking back at you

From a distance, you see me
Move much closer, what do you see?
Particles and cells, motion excelled
Speeds so quick without lenses
No one could tell

Beyond any form
Our true selves
Our bodies' cloak, our soul rebels
Seeking here, guiding fair
Until we find only God standing there

~~~
~~~

A Treasure Lives

When we expect from another
We let ourselves down
All that is fulfilling
Lives within our own hands

Projection of emotions
Distorts our clarity
Misgivings and disappointments
Come from a heart that doesn't see

All that is within, lives supreme amongst our kin
Equal with our brother, all our sisters, and beloveds
In our hearts, our very gift, of life and love and hope
In our hearts, a treasure lives, to share, to give, and float

~~~
~~~

Freedom Sings

Freedom sings
But where does it begin
In our Greater Skies

We love to hear it
But can we feel it
Living in our lives

Takes every action
To protect this sanction
Instil love in our stride

Create for others
A chance, our Brothers
To live richer lives

Freedom sings
For us to begin
Speaking up in many ways

Takes strong courage
To encourage
Freedom
Come what may

~~~
~~~

Peace

Love is the stuff we're made of
Its essence binds you and me

Our breath unites
Circles sky
Breathing land and sea

Earth rotates
To celebrate, share
Our shining sun

Night skies sparkle
Over all debacle
Peace to Everyone

~~~
~~~

It's up to Us

Waiting for things to happen
Isn't really a wait
Because we are creating
What comes to the gate

Life is a journey of creation
Destination unknown
Every step we take
Ignites a fate of its own

We are the makers
Of each moment
To do what we will
It's up to us to fill it
With brilliance
With love
With thrill

~~~
~~~

Humanity

A poem of love
And life
To share
With people everywhere

Is such a blessing
Touching others
Is giving
Hope, we really care

When I am you
And you are me
Sharing
The air we breathe

We're not separate
Together
We'll make it
In this land of humanity

~~~
~~~

Interesting feeling

Interesting feeling
The space between
Knowing, unknowing
Answers unseen

Confusing, revealing
Contemplating fate
Should I move now?
Or is now too late?

Letting go to grow
Going with the flow
Staying true to oneself
We're the arrow and the bow

The in-breath, the out-breath
Hearts beating tunes
Rising and calling
Each moment's a boon

~~~
~~~

Love Bonds

Love bonds go on and on
Its material is clear
Of kindness and golden strands
Imbued with friendliness and cheer

Love bonds are as a song
Linked by rhythm and rhyme
Every time we learn a new chime
The beat dances in time

Love bonds in life we live
Together you and I
We build a bridge; climb the ridge
En masse we touch the sky

~~~
~~~

Sunray

Those vibrations
Of great sensations
Liberating harmony

When we find them
With friends
Gold binding
Truth constantly sets us free

Feelings let us know
Intuition puts on a show
Sensitivity is the need of today

Open like a flower
Shine your light with power
Generate energy of a sunray

~~~
~~~

Being Present

What seemed worse
Was instead deemed wonderful
When it all panned out

Looked upon with soundly song
The thing we fear is often wrong
Telling lies to get along
Creating illusions… *a golden pond*

Here we are! Our time is now!
Reality *is* this holy now
As it is, nothing else with it
It simply is for us to visit

Being here, in this moment
Suddenly present, awake: we own it
Full of light, life is here
A blessing it is to consciously steer
My mind, its thoughts... to shore
Consciously living life on the ball

~~~
~~~

Expressing Life Galore

Poetry is a gift that's free
A blessing it is for you and me
To write, to read, to sing its tune
Lifting us out of any gloom

Or maybe it might just take us there
To share the feelings of despair
To reflect, to taste, to experience fate
Heavenly helps to eliminate hate

Poetry is a gift it's true
A reflection of me and you
Descriptions of our sons and lovers
Celebrates our heartfelt flutters
And deeper meanings are heaven sent
Making the heart smile, lament
Comedy included, poetry has it all
Expressing this journey of life galore

~~~
~~~

Quiet Content

A moment in meditation
Is worth a day
Of whiling every moment away

Time well spent
In no lament
Lifts our hearts
To quiet content

It is our choice
To mourn or rejoice
Ride our horse
Along our chosen course

Rein in hands
We guide our thoughts
Freeing them from self-rebuke
Picking a track
That takes us on
A joyous ride
Of kin and song

~~~
~~~

When we look closer

Beware of the dogs at the gate
Faces ferocious
Eyes of slate
Don't even try to test your fate
Best to stay clear
Of the dogs at the gate

Rearrange your life
Abate the gate
Do everything in your power
Don't give those dogs bait

Stay away, hesitate
Those dogs know how to keep you at bay
But then again
Who are they?
Are they truly, what they convey

Take a step closer, peek inside
Are those dogs even alive?
Stone structures etched with skilful hands
These dogs they come from moulded sand!

Oh my, oh my, these dogs are good
Cleverly made, it's now understood
Things are not always as they seem
When we look closer, the truth can be seen

~~~
~~~

You and me

Peace is what we're looking for
Peace is what we find
When we look inside us all
To see we are divine

It's hard to see this in our flaws
Hard to see this at all
But with open eyes, we come to adore

The love inside our humanness
A very special part
Penetrates our everyday living
Is never far apart

From each other
You and me
This love of ours
Can set us free
In this moment
Let truth be
Let's accept our divinity

~~~
~~~

Truth, Love, Joy: Our Full Glory

Our souls need to know
Truth, love, and joy
The ultimate experience
Is us
In our Full Glory

We wither
Without
Love's full expression
Could very well
Send the heart to depression

If sparks of happiness
Miss our moments
Love is wanting in some component

See, feel, act
Divine it
Create the elements
Truth, love, joy
Shine in

~~~
~~~

Each of us suffers

Sadness creates more sadness
Unhappiness creates more too
Same goes with bad feelings

Forlorn emotions should live alone

But misery loves company
Escalates the dread
Makes a party of those emotions
That should be asleep or dead

Life is already difficult
A crying shame or pain
Each of us suffers
Our melodies aren't the same

We need to lift each other up
Not curse and cuss, or blame
We need to raise each other's cup
Harmful emotions must be slain

~~~
~~~

Honesty Is

Honesty is, as honesty seems
Looks into the eyes
Its recognition gleams

Truthfulness is as action deems
Truly unable to come apart at the seams

Love is
What love is not
Easy to see … hits hard on the spot

Take a breath
Draw in deep
Which world will we live in?
In our heart's, what will we reap?

~~~
~~~

Our God Selves

Why do we do the things we do?
Create happenings
For experiences true
Knowing means nothing
Without *doing*

Coming away from this
To experience that
Brings understanding
Of where we're at

The many more angles
We perceive our true selves
Makes us greater
Closer to
Our God Selves

~~~
~~~

Busy Peace

The quest for peace
Is a busy path
Of obstacles
Distractions
And interesting companions

Peace is noisy
When we share
Love and joy
Praise our neighbours
With flair

Peace can be
When we're free
To live love with dare
To shape our fate
Let's celebrate: show our brotherly care!

~~~
~~~

Always Fly

In the void
Of non-creation
Life feels no sensation

Spark a thought
Inspire art
Lift beyond
Time in the dark

Take a step
In the unknown
Create this life
As a poem

Look up high
Through the sky
Chase our dreams
Always fly!

~~~
~~~

A Heart Opens

A heart that opens
Sends love floating
In lighter skies

Days are brighter
Nights vaster
Expansion is the prize

Worth every effort
Being brave to give it
A go every day

Gives ourselves
Life's wisdom pearls
To share along the way

~~~
~~~

All of Us

Accepting others
Is accepting oneself
Not always easy
Truth's limitless belt

Actions speak volumes
Guiding us so
Hearts are strengthened
Even small deeds grow

Never give up
Live to fill the cup
Share with others
All your luck

Embrace the good times
Sad times too
All of us living
Experience the same emotions true

~~~
~~~

Wanted

Wanted, wanted
Someone who will listen to me
Who will open my eyes
When I cannot see
Who will take my hand
And walk with me
Even if my legs
Themselves cannot see
They need to be guided
Trustingly

This someone wanted
Can be everyone you see
All of us together
Make a great family
No one should go unwanted
In this loving sea
Feeling wanted
Sets our hearts free

A wanting heart
Lives apart
Dissatisfaction is a lonely spark
It's unfulfilling and detrimental
Leaves you wanting
At every table

What is wanted is what we need
Simple consideration
In every deed

Look out to others
Offer a hand
Giving like this the heart understands

That what is wanted
Is already here
In all you good people
The meaning is clear
We must give to live
That's truly life's plan
What is wanted
Is for humans to understand

~~~
~~~

Make Hay

Missing another
It's slow to recover
The spark that lives
In the heart

But it's really still there
Just hidden, needing repair
A breath of life
Blow away despair

Rise from the covers
Step out the Beloved
Shine, create: it's your new day
Keep love alive, live life in your stride
And yes, make Hay while you stay!

~~~
~~~

True Friends

Friends so true
Come back to you
On the vine of life

They find a way
To make your day
Bringing memories
Of love and play

Friends so true
Come back to you
No, matter what you do

They find a way
Despite life's forays
To send their message
Of love that stays

~~~
~~~

Love

Love is everywhere
In me and you, lots to spare
Lifts life from despair

Love is active
Passive too
It's this
And that
Me and you

Love is the breath
I breathe
Into
A golden temple
Deep and true

Around it goes
In and out
Yet all around, some without

Why is it missing?
Forsaken too
When love is the only thing
Worth giving to

~~~
~~~

Love each other

To lose another
Is to lose ourselves
A part of us
Lost on a shelf

This loss of ours
Is it so great?
When all around
Life celebrates

Seasons come and seasons go
Rises and falls
With the ebb and the flow
To stay the same
Nature never could
No matter how we try to bend the wood

You're in me
And I'm in you
Forever apart
Yet living in cue

Kindred spirits
Never to meet
That's why I greet everyone on the street

Love each other
In all we do
Cause this life of ours
Is me and you!

~~~
~~~

Peaceful wine

Oh, peaceful wine
Lovers' ripe, essence Divine
Water-falls on earth

Where for art thou?
Peaceful wine
Brewing its wisdom
On being kind

Humans are Gems
Not a dime
To each other
We cannot be blind

Where for art thou?
God within
Uncovering you
Is not a sin

In fact, it's where we must begin
Open up wide
Let the sun shine in

~~~
~~~

Ocean of Individuality

Vast differences
Between human
Character
Ushers this world
To be

Creative and whole
So everyone can grow
Into a better you and me

Encourage each other
Raise the Beloved
Embrace humanity

Setting sail, we will never fail
On the Ocean of Individuality

~~~
~~~

Warning

Warning to all people on earth
It's time to widen our mind's girth

Regard the lilies and the trees
It's time to live with equipoise to breathe

Let's take account of people without
Mindfully share what life's all about

Consider the place that's hard to leave
Because people are living where it's no longer free
Non-living in a land of tyranny

Warning to all people on earth
It's time to begin a great rebirth

Embracing our brothers, sisters: beloveds
Let's love the world as it recovers!

~~~
~~~

Our Home Relies

Love to All
On this day of ours
To share our life with care
Together we breathe
The air, our breeze
Take in the sun so fair

Shines on us all
The golden ball
Our life-giving
Comes from rays

Non-discriminate
The sun
Is giving it
Freely
To us today

No-one owns it
We all enjoy it
Not ours to give away
With human nature
Comes the danger
Of mistakenly taking away

What's not ours
Can't sell the clouds
Do those trees belong to you?
And the water in the dams
Is it purely coming through?

All channels
Mindful panels
Are they staying true?

To the environment
Our home relies on it
Because it's me and you

~~~
~~~

To let love in

The heart needs to open
To let love in
And give of itself
Each day

Being open
Means letting love in
Shining
In your own special way

Opening is
Knocking on doors
Never turning away

It's overlooking flaws
Mine and yours
Making each other's day

~~~
~~~

Ambrosia

On the edge
Of an unknown ledge
In life that's ours
We sometimes wedge

Open our minds
To different kinds
Flavours vast in humankind

Experience this to experience that
Lessons wrought
In karmic rap

When we bring into our hearts our kin
Oh, the fruits
Of Love's Ambrosia we'll sing

~~~
~~~

Rising Renewed

Please God
Give me the strength
To do what I must do
To stay strong
On the path
I belong
Write
My life's love song

Dear God
What must I do?
To see this whole thing through
To keep the faith
Let pain dissipate
To myself I must be true

Thank you God
I know I'll get along
In this life
Allow the way
Living as one
Under the sun
Rising renewed, I will shine each day

~~~
~~~

Creating Heaven

The time has come
To shine
My sun
Over everyone

Allow the warmth
Cast it forth
Penetrate
Loving fun

No need to fear
True friends are here
False ones never stay

Shine for all
Love's a Ball
Creating
Heaven today

~~~
~~~

Not as it seems

Our eyes
Be wide
To see what's true
Open, awake
Never missing a cue

Penetrate deep
In a maze, don't sink
Question and wonder
Everything … asunder

For what we see
Is not as it seems
Our eyes need open to concealed means

Look and look; work to See
Real truth is hidden
Uncovering is free!

~~~
~~~

Handmaidens

Genuine love and self-discipline
Go deeply hand in hand
One without the other
The mind is unable to understand
Life without either two
Denotes love living on imbalanced land

True love is freedom
When these handmaidens subsist
Without them, fleeting love goes falling in an abyss

Let's muster up the courage
To live this life and give
Find within the qualities
That allow good hearts to bridge

Mind the gap
That enables flack to harmfully pour through
Find the kind that seeks Divine in Loving
Living
And *You*

~~~
~~~

Binding me and you

Best to write a poem
When I'm feeling like this
Trying to try to follow
My bliss, my bliss, my bliss

What is it I want to do?
In these moments so few
What is it that fulfils my soul?
Uncovers treasures true

Will I help others?
In what I choose to do
Can I bridge brothers?
Embracing all world's crew

Can we live for others?
As we really do
Will we know the connection?
Binding me and you

~~~
~~~

Our True Face

Here's a poem
Of sheer delight
When things are blue
Dig inside to find
The Light

It's always there
Amid the glare
Of life's calamities
People still care

About others
Not only ourselves
Especially when we realise
We're each other's pearls

Wisdom is real
When you see it reveal
A path that carries
All the way to instil

Love for others
Who are really ourselves
No separation
On this life boat

With rocky waves
At any stage
Rolling together
Our True Face is brave

~~~
~~~

Bowing Within

Always keep our hands folded from within
A humble, humble way
Bowing within
Laying our hearts to our kin
Enables us to convey
Our true story
A genuine glory
Of our lives together in sway
In the breaths we breathe
In our every deed
With each other
Let us pray

~~~
~~~

Our Wish

Colours and comfort of healing
Are fully deeply felt
Floods and streams of great goodwill
Encompass every cell

Something is released
When our minds cast a wish
Magic is dispersed
Delivering prize of specific worth

Dependent on vibration
Comes this very creation
Reliant on strong, true feeling
Attracts to you: a magnet, beacon

Neither good, nor is it bad
What has come is equal that
Thoughts conveyed. Some cause delay
To growth and progress, without it's decay

From fertile minds we abound
As little Gods, we create a sound
We must remember, remember this
This life, we're living, is as we wished

~~~
~~~

Treasure Ship

Where to find the strength?
To live my life at any length
It takes to breathe my breath
In the way that I profess

Where to find the time?
To really listen to my mind
To thine own self one must be kind
If I truly wish to help us bind

Where to find the heart?
To make a great start
On this journey, I must embark
To live this life full of spark

Where to find the passion?
To make things really happen
This life is not a cabin
It's a Treasure Ship in God's haven

Be Aware

Do we ever know ourselves?
I ask this day
Can we really discern?
Between happiness and dismay

We say we want to live in peace
Without this disarray
But how do we find such peace
The way people are living today

The western world is learning
From precious power burning
The earth's in trouble
She must grow quad double
To keep our lives this way

The developing world is catching up
We've shown just how to overload the truck
We must slow down
It's our turn to frown
Our one-pointed ways
Are devastation bound

Nature is our guide now
She's showing us the way
We must remain aware
Of what She's trying to say

~~~
~~~

Choosing Honesty

Saying the things that need to be said
Isn't easy to do
We'd rather leave them alone
Avoid an issue

Yet without the truth
Connections die
Friendships fray away

Life forces fade
When truth is denied
Choosing honesty
Saves the day

~~~
~~~

Our Heart's Steer

Find the love within
Even when without
Reflect the love that sings
Even if it's flowing
Like a leaking tap

Meditate on a waterfall
Niagara Falls will do
Let love sing evermore
Only truth is true

Its essence is overflowing
Its power knocks us out
If we're not awake to it
Get ready for an almighty clout

It'll knock us to our feet
Shake cobwebs from the mind
Give us every incentive
To be honest and wonderfully kind

We know when we have it
When we've found our heart's steer
In our waking moments
Life's purpose is very clear

~~~
~~~

Remembering my heart

We need to lose our heart
To find it again
That's what happened to me

I came undone
To find the sun
Shining in me

Un-creating myself
I saw
Myself
Standing fluid and free
Gathered the passion to refashion
A complete expression of me

~~~
~~~

Madness of indifference

The madness of misunderstanding
Oozes with unnecessary suffering

Misinterpretation and the mis-in-communication
Misses the point
Enabling preventable pain
Of frustrating strains

The only worth in striving
To find an even ground to dive in
Is when people, parties, countries
Develop a common goal uniting

A goal that is liberating
Finds no freedom in denigrating
Wings are formed deeply infiltrating

However, when a component
Behaves like an opponent
Common ground is missing, not found
Perhaps it was never there, in the darkness or the care
As humans, it seems we can be actors according to our flair

When misunderstanding grips the mind
Move backwards, sideways and forwards too
See what it is that's blocking through

And if communication can't bridge our kind
It's the madness of indifference that will hurt in time

~~~
~~~

Language of Love

The universal language of love
Is the ultimate truth
To express the God inside
Shining in
Mc and you

Any negative words or deeds
Only leads away
From the very thing
Giving precious life this day

Our actions speak
Our hearts so deep
Clearly, they convey
What is it we want to reap
What we want to say

Let us sing
To make us a grin
A smile from ear to ear
Let us do
Good
That's true
To elevate us dear

~~~
~~~

Regard Mystery

To understand life
We need recognise nature
Regard Mystery!

This life of ours
Is misunderstood
By us and all
Just take a look

We think
It's success
When people overdress
We think
It's a mess
When folks caress

What's kind is weak
What's wrong is strong
The bigger the better
The smaller; the gall
Wouldn't you want to have it all?
Great cars, large homes, TV meals all alone
Working so late; no time to hear tone

The rhythm of life
Is all mixed up
The richer have less than a full cup
It overflows and is wiped away

Sparing no thought
For others today

The nature of life
Digs deeper than strife
It births, enriches, melts away
Changes, and changes
Never the same
From one moment to the next
It remoulds a new Flame

From whence it comes
Nobody knows
Our faith tells us it's God that sows

Observe the seasons
And seeds that grow
Watch them bloom their power
Then fall even so
The soil rekindles life from them
Over and over it begins again

This life is a Mystery
To be sure
Here to be shared by one and all!

~~~
~~~

Thank you

Thank you for this moment
Shared
In an air of ease

Thank you for this work of ours
Given
Like a blessing's breeze

In trust we speak
From hearts so deep
Hail, the creative tongue!

May words we seek
Constantly peep
Insight
Into our minds
Having fun

Haiku

Deep within
where to find the dare
truly send message of care
deep within the heart

Intrinsic
life and love are one
inseparable together
flow; intrinsic dance!

Waterfall
God's water cascades
oh waterfall, quench our thirst
for peace of some kind

Happiness
precious happiness
do you really exist?
are you only in mind?

Wishing
when you wish upon
a star makes no difference who
you are. keep wishing!

To know
what is there to know
as a certainty in life?
impermanence. Change

Even alone
even when alone
matters take on a new tone
at any moment

Misunderstanding
misunderstanding;
mistaken direction fly
inner compass saves

Apologies true
apologies true
spring deep oh cavern braveheart
bridge peace and love too

Butterflies
flit butterflies flow
colour, motion, life-cycle
learning as we go!

Colour of query
colour of query
purple pastures golden hue
vast, vital green grass

Communication
communication:
build bridges near, far, high, low
pave peace the way through

Compassion
compassion reigns; frees
shackles, misery of mind
to be as it is

Dark or Light
in the dark or light
keep the beating heart open
embracing soul might

Home
loved ones, let's go home
to a place shiny and new
house of forgiveness

Free
bird lands on Palm Tree
shuffles, surveys, chirps, flies-on
living aware; Free

Humanity
life without divide
nationality: yours, mine
merge humanity!

reminding all folks!
care not the messenger; but
the message itself

Impermanence
changing sensations
fluctuating vibrations
sweep bodies en masse

Nature displays ways
nature demonstrates:
east, west, north, south, all meet
then go separate ways

One tree
the entire world
in a natural rainforest
one tree

sweet childhood friendship,
pure blossom nectar; fragrant
love to count on too

a wonderful life
full of great living loving
doing what is 'right'

thunder clouds rolling:
mind scratching its head muses
who am I this life?

peeping Tom sun plays,
lightning flash streaks across sky
tai tai tai tai Chi

synchronicity
waves and ripples ebb and flow
in perfect patterns

simultaneous:
living beings exist, breathe
moment to moment

we're never alone
our destiny is in us
to strike a new tone

on life's rocky road
find a bed of rose petals
a soft place to fall

happy party times
rock the soul, senses sublime
to love life anew

smiles of a friend
reaches deep heart crevices
helps us live again

kindred souls abound
along every destined path
lighting up the way

music opens minds
issues loving vibrations
secrets of divine

friendship gatherings
opportunities unravel
and deeper they bind

why war? stop! no more
what about the innocents
frolicking so free?

insane the pain of
war to score in freedom's name
poor people are slain

mad mad bombs are dropped
on pure civilian plots: care-
less retribution

madness came and man
went mad in the name of God
where is godly love?

hard heartedness
a splinter from the bench
wood

tears falling down the face
rain pattering the window
water

smiles shining
hearts healed
emotions

colour darting through the air
flowers beckoning
attention

sunrise
earth rotates
part by part

carelessness
an abandoned cabin
overgrown with life

juicy mangoes
the summer sunshine
running down my chin

tree trunk silhouette
woman's figure elegant
upon crimson sky

twinkle in the eyes
sun and moon meet, greet; eclipse
babies are reborn

truth enlightens love
eagle flies high in great sky
sights oyster shell's pearl

www.ingramcontent.com/pod-product-compliance
Ingram Content Group UK Ltd.
Pitfield, Milton Keynes, MK11 3LW, UK
UKHW041315190726
13845UKWH00025B/288

9 788182 531376